BRATZ BOYZ™

BOARDIN'
with the
BOYZ

GROSSET & DUNLAP · NEW YORK

Photo credits:
12: (top) Jeff Greenberg/Omni-Photo Communications, Inc.; (bottom) Jake Martin/Getty Images,
Inc./Allsport Photography. 13: (top) Joe McBride/Gettyimages; (middle) Getty Images, Inc./Photodisc;
(bottom) Carroll Seghers/Photo Researchers, Inc. 14: (left) Mike Powell/Getty Images, Inc./Allsport
Photography; (right) Mike Powell/Getty Images, Inc./Allsport Photography. 15: (bkgd) Getty Images,
Inc./Photodisc; (left) Mike Powell/Getty Images, Inc./Allsport Photography; (middle) Carroll
Seghers/Photo Researchers, Inc.; (right) Joe McBride/Gettyimages. 16: Jake Martin/Getty Images,
Inc./Allsport Photography. 17: (top) Joe McBride/Gettyimages; (bottom left) Getty Images,
Inc./Photodisc; (bottom right) Lawrence Migdale/Pix. 18: (top to bottom) Getty Images/Photodisc;
Joe McBride/Gettyimages; Mike Powell/Getty Images, Inc./Allsport Photography; Bob Shaw/AP/Wide
World Photos. 19: Mike Powell/Getty Images, Inc./Allsport Photography. 20: (top) Jake Martin/Getty
Images, Inc./Allsport Photography; (bottom) Lawrence Migdale/Pix. 23: Mike Powell/Getty Images,
Inc./Allsport Photography. 30: (top) Getty Images, Inc./Photodisc; (middle) Joe McBride/Gettyimages;
(bottom) Mike Powell/Getty Images, Inc./Allsport Photography. 31: (left) Mike Powell/Getty Images,
Inc./Allsport Photography; (middle) Carroll Seghers/Photo Researchers, Inc.; (right) Jake
Martin/Getty Images, Inc./Allsport Photography.

www.bratzpack.com
TM & © 2004 MGA Entertainment, Inc. Bratz and all related logos, names and
distinctive likenesses are the exclusive property of MGA Entertainment, Inc.
All Rights Reserved.

Used under license by Penguin Young Readers Group. Published by Grosset & Dunlap, a division
of Penguin Young Readers Group, 345 Hudson Street, New York, New York 10014.
GROSSET & DUNLAP is a trademark of Penguin Group (USA) Inc. Printed in the U.S.A.

Library of Congress Cataloging-in-Publication Data
Boardin' with the Boyz.
p. cm. — (Bratz Boyz)
ISBN 0-448-43626-4 (pbk.)
1. Skateboarding—Juvenile literature. I. Title: Boarding with the Boys. II. Bratz Boyz (Series)
GV859.8.B63 2004
796.22—dc22
2004002120

ISBN 0-448-43626-4   10 9 8 7 6 5 4 3 2 1

HI! **CAMERON**™ HERE! MY BOYS CALL ME "THE BLAZE" BECAUSE I'M SO FAST, I'M ON FIRE! WE LOVE HANGIN' WITH OUR FRIENDS, AND WE HAVE A PASSION FOR CUTTING-EDGE ADVENTURE AND XTREME SPORTS! AND WHILE WE LOVE ALL OF OUR FRIENDS, OUR FAVORITE THING TO DO IS TO KICK BACK AND CHILL OUT— JUST THE BOYS!

YO! **CADE**™ COMIN' AT YA! YOU CAN CALL ME "THE VIPER" 'CAUSE I'M THE SHARPEST THING AROUND. I LOVE TO TAKE MY BIKE OUT FOR XTREME ADVENTURES!

W'SUP! I'M **EITAN**.™ MY BOYS CALL ME "THE DRAGON" 'CAUSE I'M A NONSTOP HOTSHOT! WHEN I'M NOT OUT WITH THE CREW HAVING XTREME ADVENTURES, I LIKE TO READ COMICS AND WATCH JAPANIMATION, BUT I'M ALWAYS UP FOR NEW ADVENTURES.

KOBY™ HERE. I LOVE TO DO ALL KINDS OF SPORTS. AND I DIG MAKING COOL MOVIES WITH MY VIDEO CAMERA. SOMETIMES I GO BY "THE PANTHER" BECAUSE I'M ALWAYS ON THE PROWL!

I'M **DYLAN**.™ BUT YOU CAN CALL ME "THE FOX" BECAUSE I'M SO SLICK. I LOVE HIP-HOP MUSIC—AND I LOVE TO DRESS IN HIP-HOP STYLES!

Xtreme sports

AS YOU CAN SEE, MY BOYS ARE ALWAYS INTO TRYING OUT NEW SPORTS AND GAMES. I'M WAY INTO BOARDIN', AND I'M GOING TO TELL YOU ALL ABOUT IT! GET PSYCHED!

safety tips

BEFORE YOU BEGIN

Well, you already know that boardin' rules! If you like what you read here, you should *definitely* try it out! But if you're gonna board, it's important to play by the rules and be safe:

✳ If you're going to go out to practice your boardin', let your parents or another adult know where you are going to be.

✳ Dress comfortably in loose clothing and sneakers—but stick to light, bright colors, and always practice in the daytime, away from traffic.

✳ *Always* wear protective gear—helmets, and wrist, knee, and elbow pads. A bad wipeout could keep you off of your board for a long time!

Did You Know?

BOARDIN' AS WE KNOW IT BEGAN IN 1958 WITH SURFERS IN SOUTHERN CALIFORNIA. THEY WERE LOOKING FOR A WAY TO SURF ON LAND ON DAYS WHEN THEY COULDN'T CATCH A WAVE. THEY ATTACHED WHEELS TO SMALL PLANKS OF WOOD, AND HIT THE BOARDWALKS. IT WASN'T LONG BEFORE TOY MANUFACTURERS CAUGHT ON TO THE TREND AND SOON—BOARDIN' WAS BORN!

BOARDIN' BASICS

Skateboards may have started as one wooden plank attached to some wheels, but these days, the design has been amped up for the ultimate riding experience! Instead of a flat board, designers like to create two **concaves** (curves) at either end of the **deck** (the wooden surface of the board that riders stand on). The concave at the front of your deck is called the **nose**, and the concave at the back of your deck is called the **tail**. These concaves strengthen the board and give the rider more control.

AWESOME!

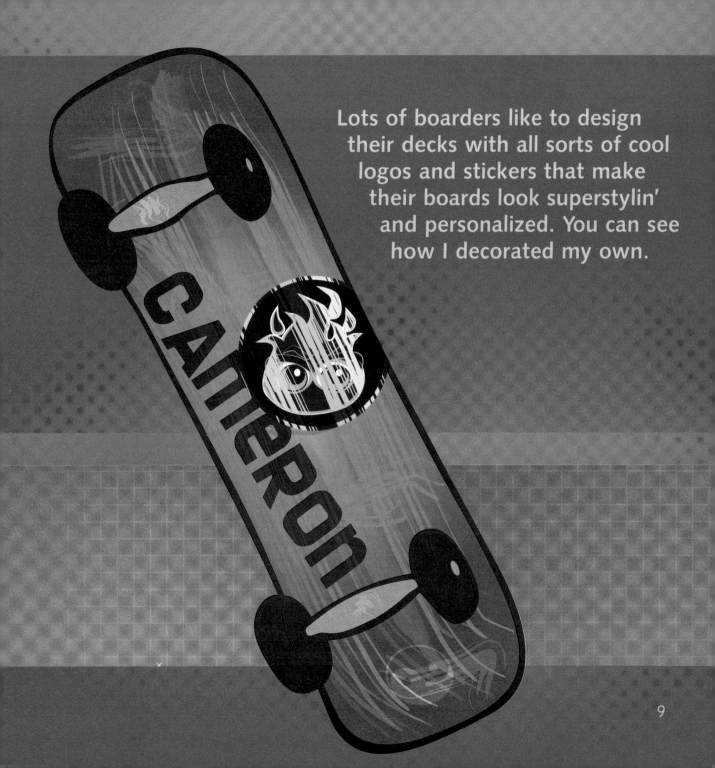

Lots of boarders like to design their decks with all sorts of cool logos and stickers that make their boards look superstylin' and personalized. You can see how I decorated my own.

the gear

Well, the first thing you need to board is your board! Your deck is the part of your board that gets the most notice, but other things like the **wheels**, **axle** (the pin on which the wheel revolves), **bearings** (small metal balls in the wheels that help them spin), and **grip tape** (the rough sheet of sandpaper attached to the deck that helps your feet stay gripped to the board) are very important to your ride too! It's key to keep your board in top condition for the smoothest possible ride.

When you first start practicing, you're gonna wipe out—a *lot*! It happens to all of us, especially when we're trying a new trick. Don't worry about it—but *do* keep yourself safe with lots of protective gear, like helmets and special pads. Trust me—you don't want to fall without them!

the garb

There's no rule to boardin' style—just cool, comfort-able, cutting-edge fashion. You should wear whatever makes you feel best when you practice. Lots of boarders like to skate casual-cool in baggy cargo pants or jeans, layers of T-shirts (so you can remove a layer if you get hot), and sneakers.

boardin' 101

First, you'll want to figure out your **stance**. The two basic skateboarding stances are **normal** (left foot forward on the board) and **goofy** (right foot forward on the board). It's easy to figure out which is your stance—the foot you would naturally use to kick a soccer ball will be the foot that stays on the back end of your board. You will sometimes place it on the ground to **pump** (push off and propel yourself forward). Once you've figured out your stance, you should spend some time getting used to the feel of the board beneath your feet. It will take a little while to get comfortable enough to try out tricks—so don't get too frustrated, and don't give up!
You'll get it!

Fun Fact:

EARLY BOARDERS HAD A PRETTY SIMPLE GOAL—START AT THE TOP OF THE HILL AND RIDE DOWN. STAYING ON AND AVOIDING A WIPEOUT WAS A BIG ENOUGH CHALLENGE! NOW, THANKS TO IMPROVEMENTS IN BOARD DESIGN, MOST RIDERS HAVE A HIGHER CALLING, AND LIKE TO TRY OUT DIFFERENT STUNTS! SOON YOU'LL BE READY TO TRICK OUT (DO STUNTS) TOO!

where to board

Basically, all you really need is a wide, open space. But remember that you should *never* go out boardin' without telling your parents or another adult where you're going to be. Public spaces like parking lots or outdoor staircases make good practice areas, but *only* when no cars—or people who aren't boardin' with you—are around!

🌀 **Your own driveway:** This is the most obvious place to go, since you'll know right off the bat whether you'll be in anyone's way. Driveways are generally long and flat, so you have lots of space to **cruise** (coast along casually, getting the feel for your board)—great for beginners.

🌀 **Hills:** Before they started practicing hardcore stunts, experienced skaters just wanted to get down a hill in one piece. Not a bad goal for a beginner! Your neighborhood probably has some hills around that you can check out—start small and *stay away from traffic*.

🌀 **Your neighborhood park:** Many parks and play-grounds have lots of safe, paved areas—including longer, winding paths and also slants and ramps that will help you pick up speed more safely than you might on a hill.

13

tricking out

Here are some popular skateboard tricks:

Switch stance: This is riding with your opposite stance. For example, if you normally ride regular, you would try to ride goofy, and vice versa.

Fakie: Riding backward (in your normal stance).

Grind: Scraping one or both axles on a curb, railing, or other surface.

Air: Riding with all four wheels off the ground; short for aerial.

Ollie: A jump performed by tapping the tail of the board on the ground; the basis of most skating tricks.

Nollie: Tapping the nose of the board down instead of the tail, like a reverse ollie.

Nosegrind: Grinding with only the front axle.

Railslide: A trick in which the skater slides the underside of the deck along an object, such as a curb or handrail.

I have a passion for boardin' and, naturally, I do it in style. But ya know, even the pros have their off days—and that includes yours truly! So there I was, just a few weeks ago, sportin' my superstylin' new skate sneakers and carrying my brand-new board. I bought one with a special short **deck** like the pros use for **tricking out** (shorter boards are less useful for a casual boarder, but a shorter deck can give you more control of the board). I was practicing outside of school on a Saturday 'cause I figured no one would be around—not that I mind an audience!

Anyway, I can do an awesome **ollie**, so I thought I'd try a **nollie**. I started off with some **nosegrinds** until I felt ready. I started at the top of a staircase, and caught some serious **air**!

The problem was when I came down.

It wasn't a smooth landing. Hardly! It was a total and complete wipeout!

Well, usually I'm a big believer in getting right back on the horse, but this time . . . well, I hate to admit it, but who should come out of the school but my friend Cloe™? I guess she was working on some special project, but she saw every-thing. She didn't laugh at me—but I could tell she wanted to! How embarrassing!

skateparks intro

There are four different kinds of boardin' that the pros practice:

Street skating: Skating on streets, curbs, benches, handrails, and other places found in most neighborhoods.

Vert skating: Skating on ramps and other vertical structures specifically designed for skating.

Half-pipe: A U-shaped ramp of any size, usually with a flat section in the middle.

Vert ramp: A half-pipe, usually at least eight feet tall, with steep sides that are perfectly vertical near the top.

Street skating is the type you'll probably be practicing most, because you don't need to go anywhere special to do it (make sure Mom and Dad know where you are and what you're up to!). Vert skating and half-pipe tricks can really only be done in specially designed skateparks. But there are lots of parks out there across the globe, so if you're dyin' to test your skillz, get packin'!

top skateparks

Here are just a few of the places for you to get your skate on in the US. Check the web because new parks open all the time!

Alameda, CA: Alameda Skatepark
A great free park in the heart of the San Francisco Bay area. This park was created by local skaters who got together to raise funds for its construction. How's that for teamwork?

Houston, TX: Sun City Skatepark
This 17,000-square-foot facility features two mini ramps—a three-and-a-half-foot and a seven-foot—as well as beginner and intermediate street courses. Pads are required—you might get fined if you leave yours behind!—and you do need to pay to get in the park.

New York, NY: Chelsea Piers Skatepark
This park is actually part of an enormous sports complex housed in a refurbished warehouse! We're guessing you're gonna want to board all day, but if not, there are tons of other activities to try out, like blading, batting, swimming, and more!

Lynnwood, WA: Griffith Skatepark
This park includes a street course with bowl, hips, two ledges, two banks, and quarter-pipe, and it's free to the skating public!

Did You Know:

THE X GAMES HAVE ONE FEATURE COMPETITION CALLED VERT DOUBLES WHERE BOARDERS PICK PARTNERS AND CREATE HALF-PIPE ROUTINES. IF THE TEAM'S TIMING IS OFF BY JUST A LITTLE, THE BOARDERS COULD COLLIDE, RISK INJURY, AND RUIN THEIR RUN. TEAMWORK IS PRETTY IMPORTANT—IN BOARDING, JUST LIKE IN LIFE!

competitions

Today, many skate competitions are held every year and for every level of skating ability. One of the earliest and best-known competitions is the X Games.

The X Games were created by the sports television network ESPN in 1995 because Xtreme sports were becoming so popular. Xtreme sports include BMX biking, motocross, snowboarding, in-line skating (or blading), street luge, and, of course, skateboarding!

At the X Games, athletes compete for medals and hope to become the best in their Xtreme sports. But along with the glory comes risk—athletes are always trying to keep from *wiping* out when they're *tricking* out!

EITAN HERE. WHEN I'M HANGIN' ON MY OWN, I'M WAY INTO COMICS, JAPANIMATION, AND COOL VIDEO GAMES. BUT THAT DOESN'T MEAN I DON'T LIKE TO GET OUTSIDE AND GO XTREME WITH MY BOYS! WHEN I SAW CAMERON PRACTICING HIS LATEST TRICKS WITH HIS BOARD, I KNEW I HAD TO TRY BOARDIN'.

I WAS SO PSYCHED WHEN EITAN
ASKED ME TO TEACH HIM TO BOARD!
I'VE NEVER SHOWN ANYONE HOW TO
SKATE BEFORE, BUT WHAT ARE FRIENDS
FOR? ANYWAY, SINCE I JUST BOUGHT
MY NEW SHORT BOARD, I LENT EITAN
MY REGULAR SKATEBOARD, AND
WE HIT THE STREETS!

23

YO! SO, EITAN AND I DECIDED TO PRACTICE HARD, AND WE TOOK OUR BOARDS OUT EVERY AFTERNOON. WE HAD SOME SPILLS, BUT AFTER A LITTLE WHILE, EITAN WAS GRINDIN'! MY BOY ROCKED!

ONCE YOU'VE GOTTEN A HANDLE ON CRUISING, YOU CAN MOVE ON TO THE OLLIE. THE OLLIE IS THE MOST BASIC SKATEBOARD TRICK. WHEN PERFORMING IT, A BOARDER TAPS THE TAIL OF HIS BOARD ON THE GROUND WITH HIS BACK FOOT, WHICH FORCES THE BOARD INTO THE AIR. THE BOARD IS BALANCED WITH THE FRONT FOOT. THE BOARD LOOKS LIKE IT'S STUCK TO THE RIDER'S FEET AS HE OR SHE GETS SOME SERIOUS AIR. MOST SKATEBOARD TRICKS HAVE EVOLVED FROM A BASIC OLLIE.

Did You Know:

THE OLLIE WAS CREATED BY ALAN "OLLIE" GELFAND.

skateboard science

When a boarder pulls off an amazing ollie, it looks like he or she is actually connected to the deck. But that's not true at all! And what's even weirder is that to get the skateboard to jump up, the skater pushes *down* on the board! Believe it or not, this is because of the rules of physics.

Try it and see!

practice

EITAN'S OLLIE WAS SO AWESOME THAT WE DECIDED HE WAS READY TO COMPETE TO THE XTREME! HE WAS A LITTLE NERVOUS 'CAUSE HE'S NEW TO BOARDIN', BUT WE CONVINCED HIM THAT HE WAS READY!

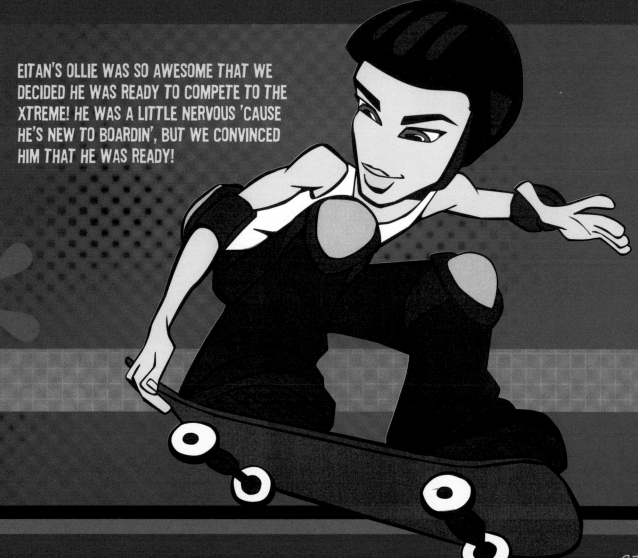

WE ALL THOUGHT EITAN WOULD BE A LITTLE NERVOUS ON THE DAY OF THE COMPETITION, BUT MY BOY WAS COOL, AS ALWAYS.

WHAT I DIDN'T KNOW WAS THAT HE HAD BEEN PRACTICING **EXTRA**, WHEN I WASN'T EVEN AROUND!

SO WE WERE ALL STOKED WHEN WE SAW HIM PULL AN XTREME MOVE: A **NOLLIE OVER TO A FRONTSIDE GRIND!** (HINT: CHECK THE GLOSSARY OF SKATER SLANG ON THE NEXT PAGE AND YOU'LL KNOW EXACTLY HOW COOL HIS MOVES WERE!)

EITAN CAME IN THIRD PLACE! PRETTY EXCELLENT FOR A FIRST-TIMER!

glossary

If you've been paying attention, you've definitely picked up on some of the skating slang we've been using! But just in case, here's a recap—*and*, just for good measure, some bonus extra terms for you!

air: riding with all four wheels off the ground; short for aerial

axle: the pin on which the skateboard wheels revolve

bail: pull out of a trick early to avoid losing control of the board (trust us, we've *all* done this!)

barge: skating in places where boardin' isn't allowed
(we've never done this!)

bearings: small metal balls in the wheels that help them spin

concaves: curves at either end of the skateboard deck; for example, the nose and the tail

deck: the wooden surface of the skateboard that riders stand on

fakie: riding backward (in your normal stance)

flatland: a form of street skating in which tricks are performed on the pavement without other obstacles like stairs or curbs

go big: perform a trick either high in the air, over a large area or distance, or off a verrrry tall surface—in other words, supersizin' your stunt

goofy stance: right foot forward on the board

grind: scraping one or both axles on a curb, railing, or other surface

grip tape: the rough sheet of sandpaper attached to the deck that helps your feet stay gripped to the board

half-pipe: a U-shaped ramp of any size, usually with a flat section in the middle

nollie: tapping the nose of the board down instead of the tail; a reverse ollie

normal stance: left foot forward on the board

nose: the front concave of the deck

nosegrinds: grinding only with the front axle

ollie: a jump performed by tapping the tail of the board on the ground; the basis of most skating tricks

railslide: sliding the underside of the deck along an object like a curb or handrail

slam: a fall that usually results in injury

street skating: skating on streets, curbs, benches, handrails, and other places found in most neighborhoods

switch stance: riding with your opposite stance

tail: the back concave of the deck

trick out: to do stunts

tweak: to move your body during a trick

vert ramp: a half-pipe, usually at least eight feet tall, with steep sides that are perfectly vertical near the top

vert skating: skating on ramps and other vertical structures specifically designed for skating

OF COURSE, EITAN GETS FIRST PLACE IN FRIENDSHIP FROM ALL OF THE BOYS! NOW HE'S BOARDIN' TO THE XTREME—AND WE HOPE YOU WILL BE TOO!